Cricut Maker for Beginners

Learn How to Use Your Cutting
Machine Starting From Zero and Make
Money with it. Cricut for Beginners
Guide with Easy to Follow Illustrated
Examples for DIY Project Ideas

Jessie Crafts

This book may contain advices, opinions and statements from various information providers. It does not represent or endorse the accuracy or reliability of the suggestions, opinions, declarations or other information provided by any information provider, any reader or any other person or entity. Trust in any advice, opinion, statement or other information will also be at the risk and expense of the reader. Neither the owner nor the author will be responsible to the reader or any other person for any inaccuracy, error, omission, interruption, elimination, defect, alteration or use of any content in this document, or for its timeliness or integrity.

Table of Contents

Cricut Projects for Beginners..................66

Tips of Making Money Using Cricut.... 108

Introduction

The Cricut machine is the last cutting machine released from the Cricut Company which had already made itself known for the Cricut Explore among others. The Cricut Maker is a plotter that can both cut various materials and write / draw on them, it can also perforate them (create those tear lines typical of cinema tickets, so to speak), engrave them (for example Plexiglas and aluminum), create reliefs (such as in the case of embossing, even if in this house it is actually a debossing) or even folding lines (very useful if you make cards, tickets, boxes, etc.).

The machine will do one or the other depending on the accessory (blade, tip or pen) that we are using. This machine is the Rolls Royce of cutting machines. And for good reason! Imagine any media up to 3mm thick, the machine will cut it with ten times the power of the Cricut Explore and its other competitors. What made me fall for this machine is the possibility of cutting leather.

The Cricut machine can cut cardboard, balsa, vinyl, flex, burlap (!)… And FABRIC. Yes! You read that right fabric! And not just cotton! Not all kinds of fabric imaginable! In the Design Space you can find all kinds of fabrics: velvet, jersey, silk, lace! In all, the Maker cuts around 100 different materials up to 3mm thick. Another important feature of the Maker: you can write with it!

Whatever the type of material we want to work with the maker (paper, wood, jeans ...), we will have to introduce it in the machine after making it adhere on special reusable mats , mats that are equipped with a more or less resistant layer of glue : if we are using paper we will use a mat with a layer of not very resistant glue, if instead we are using wood we will use a mat with a much more powerful layer of glue. There are four mats available:

1) light blue (Light Grip Mat), ideal for standard paper, light cardboard and parchment
2) green (Standard Grip Mat), suitable for heavy cardstock, printed paper, vinyl and iron-on vinyl.
3) purple (Strong Grip Mat), to be used with special cardboard, chipboard, cardboard and other heavy materials and
4) Pink (Fabric Grip) to be used with most fabrics, including cotton, polyester, denim, felt and canvas.

The Cricut machine has a double carriage allowing two operations to be carried out in a single pass. It is thus possible to draw (or use the "scoring tool "to make folds) and cut at the same time.

As on the Cricut Explore, an optical drive allows for Print & Cut. This has however been improved because it is now possible to perform a Print & Cut on colored or patterned paper.

As Cricut now favors the sale of patterns online, the Cricut Maker does not have a port to use pattern cartridges. To overcome the criticisms of their loyal customers, the American brand has designed a USB adapter (sold separately) to import the patterns of the cartridges into the Design Space software.

The machine does not have an LCD screen, which can be confusing at first. But, considering that this one only displayed little on previous machines, users might think that the machine was limited to these few uses. The engineers at Cricut therefore decided to remove the screen to show that this machine was not limited in terms of capacity.

Cricut also emphasizes the unlimited potential of the Cricut Maker as well as its scalability. Indeed, the machine should accept in the future all future accessories that Cricut will market.

In terms of storage, we can note 2 locations for storing unused blades, pencils or other small accessories. The Cricut Maker is rightly considered the Rolls Roys from Cricut! You will never feel like you are limited by this machine because of the many possibilities it is able to offer you. If you sew, you will no longer cry to tear your fabrics thanks to the 2 dedicated blades (rotating + special coated fabric blade). The price can be a drag for some, however this is a tough and versatile machine that you will keep for a long time. We must therefore consider this as a long-term investment. The Cricut Maker is a machine that you will not disappoint and that you will use for many years to come.

Reasons of Choosing Cricut

1. NOISE LEVEL

This was the main reason that kept me from choosing the Silhouette. Although Cricut is not a silent machine, the cameo sounds so loud and weird that it bothers me. Some will say it's a matter of habit, but that sound is a BIG NOT to me. On YouTube there is a video where it shows the speed and sound of both machines.

2. USE OF VECTORS (SVG)

Without having to pay an extra cost I can use SVG files. I am aware of Adobe Illustrator, so the software is a bit limited is not a problem for me. If you don't use Adobe Illustrator the Cricut software is a limitation.

3. I DON'T DEPEND ON MY PC TO WORK

Something that really caught my attention was the ability to use my machine from my cell phone or iPad. For example, I am in the waiting room for the doctor designing something that I have to work from the comfort of my cell phone, since when I get home I only need to press the GO button without even connecting or having to transfer the file to my PC.

4. SMART ADJUSTMENT WHEEL

With a simple turn of the wheel, I can do my projects much faster. This wheel has the settings for the 7 most common materials and a fit between two materials that increases my cutting depth in case the material is a little thicker than normal.

5. EASY TO USE

It has made this machine so simple to use that those who have never done anything creative can use it. It is a simple design, place your mat and press the GO button. The software places the shapes on each mat, differentiating whether it is something to print, cut and what color is intended for each design. The most difficult decision is to determine which material to cut each shape.

6. CAPACITY WITH DIFFERENT MATERIALS

From a line of washitape, cardboard, foami, balsa wood, fabric and many more. If it can be placed under the rollers, this machine can cut it. With my Engineering mind, I needed numbers and proof that this is true; And I found a study done by an independent lab that tested the precision, strength and cutting ability between the Silhouette Cameo and the Cricut Explore Air.

7. MORE PRECISE CUT IN MORE DETAILED DESIGNS

Another reason why I decided to use the Cricut is why it can make smaller, more precise cuts. In the little time I have with my machine I have already cut a complete sentence for the cover of an IPhone 8, where I distrusted the machine thinking that I could not make those small cuts. And by surprise, he did it without problems! Below is a picture of how the design looks.

8. MACHINE DESIGN

The design of the Cricut I love how it looks, the colors (although the cameo has some beautiful pastel colors too), design, etc. Although we should not judge a machine by its cover, there is no doubt that aesthetics are important, especially if it is something that will be in your work area all day.

9. BOOKMARK ADAPTER

The Cricut marker cart can be used with different markers, not just those of the brand, since they have a traditional design not like those of Silhouette which are quite small and chubby.

10. ¨MAKE IT NOW¨ PROYECTOS PROJECTS

In Cricut's design space there is a category where you find complete projects where you only need to get the materials. The software indicates the materials, colors, working time, level of knowledge (whether advanced or beginner) up to the indications. Look at this beautiful detail for Valentine's Day, it's just a matter of looking for the materials, press GO and follow the instructions.

Contents of The Box

- **The Cricut Maker Machine**. I think the designers have done a really good job of keeping this machine 10x more powerful than its predecessors to remain a work of art. The rounded design, the colorful cover, these are details that make you love just opening it!

Two specific points: there are now two storage locations and you have a groove to store your tablets / smartphone because the machine can connect to your devices via Bluetooth! When unpacking I was impressed with the weight of the machine! 5.1kg: a beautiful baby isn't it. It may seem strange but for me the weight of a machine is a sign of its robustness. When you see the 2kg cacailles on the market, I doubt their pressure force when cutting. Indeed, it is the pressure of the 4kg blade that will allow you to cut your material deeply and without moving the project.

- **The** Rotary Blade + the assembly cover
- **The fine-point blade** (Premium Fine-Point Blade) + the assembly cover

With these two boards you can already clearly have fun on hundreds of projects prepared in the Design Space or that you create yourself. Personally, I fell in love with the Cutter blade

(*Knife Blade*) which cuts leather, the deep blade (*the Deep Point Blade*) that I used before the release of the Cutter blade and the *scoring wheels* (a and two)) but I haven't tried them yet (yes, I do - sometimes - accidentally buy). I sincerely think that for the set-up and the first projects, the blades included in the starter box are fine.

Fine Point Pen, Black. It is possible to write with the Maker. So, the point pen is available in 30 different colors.

- **Mat Fabric** , 12 " x 12 " (30.5 cm x 30.5 cm)
- **Light Grip** Mat, 12 " x 12 " (30.5cm x 30.5cm)

The two rugs that come with the Cricut are super useful! The fabric mat (pink) allows you to cut… fabric, amazing isn't it? And the second mat, blue is the standard mat that I personally use for all my cutouts except thick materials: leather, cardboard. For these I got the strong adherent mat (purple colour). I had a lot of doubts about the longevity of my rugs. I had read reviews for other cutting machines that the carpet no longer adhered after the third or fourth cut. Here, I am over a hundred cut-out projects completed (all materials combined) and had to clean my high-grip mat twice and the fabric mat once. In a future article I will give you my tips for cleaning and preserving these rugs.

- **The welcome book**. This book supplied with the machine is currently in English but this article contains the points to remember

- **The USB cable**: which is long enough, the pc must not stick to the machine as it needs room to make the cutouts.

- **The power outlet**. The Cricut Maker set and EU adapter included in it.

Cricut Summary Table

	Cricut Maker
Maximum cutting width	29.2 cm
Maximum cutting length	Up to 56.2 cm with the large mat - 29.2 cm with the standard carrier sheet
Cutting force	4000 g
Digitization	No
Drawing	Yes
Print & Cut	Yes

LCD touch screen	No
Supported file types	svg, png, dxf, gif, bmp, jpg
Connections	USB + Bluetooth
Guarantee	2 years manufacturer

Types of Cricut Machines

Following are different kinds of Circuit Machines:

Cricut Explore Air

Description

Cut and write up to 2X faster than previous Cricut Explore models with this DIY speed machine. The Cricut Explore Air cuts over 100 materials — everything from cardstock, vinyl and iron-on to specialty materials like glitter paper, cork, and bonded fabric. Quickly. Beautifully. From cards to custom T-shirts to home decor, Cricut makes it easy to realize your creative vision. Design on the go on your laptop, iPad or iPhone. Browse and play with thousands of images, fonts, and ready-to-make projects. Or create your own design from scratch.

Features

- This DIY speed machine combines time-saving performance and class-leading simplicity
- Cuts 100 materials – everything from cardstock, vinyl, and iron-on to a range of specialty materials

- Fine-Point Blade for cutting a wide variety of popular craft materials
- Fast Mode for up to 2X faster cutting and writing
- Bluetooth wireless technology
- Compatible with Scoring Stylus and Deep-Point Blade
- Double tool holder to keep blade and pen always at the ready
- Design Space software for iOS, Android, Windows, and Mac
- Upload and use your own images and fonts for free
- Compatible with Cricut cartridges

Included

- Cricut Explore Air machine
- Premium Fine-Point Blade + Housing
- Fine Point Pen, Black
- LightGrip Mat, 12" x 12" (30.5 cm x 30.5 cm)
- Welcome Book
- USB cable
- Power adapter
- 50 ready-to-make projects

- Materials for a practice project

Cricut Maker & Cricut Explor Air 2

Both have a very similar physical appearance but the big difference is the cutting power that each one has and the adaptive tool system that only the Cricut Maker has allowing you to change the blade without having to change the casing.

The Cricut Explore Air 2 allows you to cut more than 100 types of materials from cardboard to vinyl but it has a cutting force of 400gr, a much lower figure than that of the Maker. It lets you cut materials up to 2.4mm thick thanks to its 4kg cutting force.

What does this mean? That the Cricut Maker allows you to cut many more materials such as balsa wood, chipboard, leather, etc. It has a special blade to cut thicker materials, the Knife Blade. Thanks to its gear system, it allows greater control of cutting tools, being able to cut materials with greater precision and force.

The Explore Air 2 has a dial on the machine itself where you can select the material you are going to cut or you can put it in

«Custom» to choose the material from Design Space. Instead, in Maker you choose it directly from the application.

The Cricut Maker has a much broader tool pack than the Explore, such as the Scoring Wheel that allows you to perform much more precise marking, the engraving knife, the wave knife, the drilling knife and the debossing knife.

Plus, it lets you cut fabric with the rotary blade that's already included in the Cricut Maker box without the need to purchase the stabilized fabric blade as you need for the Explore.

What conclusion do we draw with all this? If your projects are based on vinyl or thin cardboard, the Cricut Explore Air 2 is the best solution, but if you want to go a little further, definitely buy the Cricut Maker.

Cricut Joy

It has a mini size that allows you to store it in any corner of your house and even transport it from one place to another in a simple way.

You can both cut and draw as with the other plotters but with a maximum width of 11 cm. The big difference with the others is that it has a single car. Both the blade and the markers are placed in the same place, you have to change the accessory as you want to cut or draw.

Another of the great novelties is that it incorporates a new special card mat. You can cut folded cards, the machine will cut only the top layer and you can put cardboard with effects underneath.

Yes, finally what we all wanted has arrived, to be able to cut without a mat. It can cut 10 cm wide and 1 meter long but can repeat vinyl cuts up to 6 meters long.

What types of materials do you cut?

The most common, which are not extremely thick, such as textile vinyl, adhesive vinyl, cardboard, paper and adhesive paper. If we try to cut much thicker materials we could break the machine since it is not made for it.

It has no button, you have to connect via Bluetooth. You can use it perfectly from your mobile or tablet through the Design Space app. If you want to work with the PC, it will have to have Bluetooth, otherwise it will not work. It is the easiest cutting plotter to use, perfect for doing small last minute projects.

Why buy the Cricut Joy?

Many people already have another bigger plotter and they end up buying the Cricut Joy too because it is the most practical thing on the market. You save time, it doesn't make any noise and you can take it anywhere with you.

In conclusion, it is the perfect cutting plotter for people who have none or as a complement to the big ones.

What does it include when you buy it?

- The Cricut Joy machine
- Knife + knife holder
- 0.4mm black marker pen
- Normal adhesion mat 11.4 x 16.5 cm
- Welcome book
- Power adapter
- Free trial for Cricut Access (only for new subscribers)
- 50 free projects
- Sample materials for a first test

Cricut with Infusible Ink Transfer

Basically they are sheets with a special ink that when ironing transfers the cut design to the product. You can choose between those that have a predetermined pattern or a single color. It has a slightly thicker texture than normal textile or adhesive vinyl sheets, but then the touch disappears when the garment is ironed, since what is transferred is only the ink.

Circut's new Infusible Ink system offers professional quality transfers, integrating ink into the material. Due to this process, the durability is that of the material itself, so the design does not crack, nor does it ever peel off with the passage of time and washing.

Create T-shirts, bags or objects with powerful pops of color and very sharp. All this in three simple steps: choose the material, make the design and apply the heat

They are available in the following packages:

- Pack 4 Pattern sheets
- Pack 2 Pattern sheets
- Pack 2 Solid sheets

Keep in mind that once you iron the colors are much more vibrant than when you see it on the sheet itself where the color is more muted.

The newest are the Infusible Ink markers with which you draw on a sheet by hand or put it in the Maker or Explore Air 2 and then iron it on the chosen product. It allows you to do this thanks to the ink that is included in the pen.

Remember that if you do it by hand and write it, you should write it in mirror mode, otherwise when you iron it it will be read backwards. There are two thicknesses: 0.4mm or 1.0mm

In addition, you must put silicone paper to protect the product.

You don't need such large machinery to customize!

What fabrics can you personalize with the Infusible Ink collection?

Must be polyester. The brand itself has launched a line of products to work with Infusible Ink: men's and women's t-shirts, tote bags and coasters.

Follow the next procedure:

- Choose the item you want to customize, it must be suitable for use with Infusible Ink, not just any product.
- Choose the Infusible Ink sheet
- Cut the design you want with a mirror cutting plotter
- Remove the excess material with a peeler
- Iron at 205° for 40 seconds

Cricut Installation

Cricut Design Space can be installed on your Mac or Windows computer or as an application on your iOS or Android device. Please review the recommended minimum system requirements to ensure that your device will be compatible with Cricut Design Space software. Machines Cricut Explore and Cricut Maker are the recommended minimum system requirements for use. All Cricut smart cutting machines come with Design Space. Occasionally, the recommended minimum system requirements for Cricut machines and Design Space software and applications may change to improve software performance while operating system updates are met. As software and application

Basic Toolkit

These essential tools are all you need for a craft session with Cricut.

Scissors

Cricut Scissors have hardened stainless steel blades for durability and smooth, even cuts. The micro tip blade gives you greater precision on all materials. A removable sheath protects the blades.

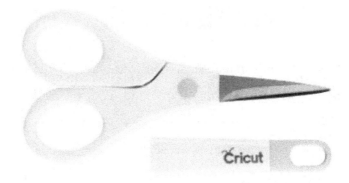

Grippers

Cricut Grippers lift and secure in one step with their reverse grip design: squeeze the handle to open them and release any pressure to close them. Smooth interior dots help prevent tearing or damage to your materials.

Escardillo

The escardillo Cricut is for "weed" or eliminate negative pieces around a cut image. When working with heat-adhesive vinyl images, it helps you to accurately remove everything that is not part of your backing sheet design. It is also ideal for removing small negative pieces from a cut cardboard image.

Scraper / Scraper XL

The Cricut Scraper is custom designed to clean up unwanted debris from Cricut cutting mats, contributing to a more durable mat. It can also be used to smooth materials on the mat or polish materials such as vinyl to remove air bubbles or wrinkles.

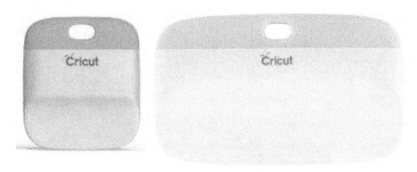

Spatula

The Cricut Spatula accurately lifts images off the Cricut cutting mat and thus prevents complex images from tearing or folding. The angled spatula head allows you to slide underneath the material with ease.

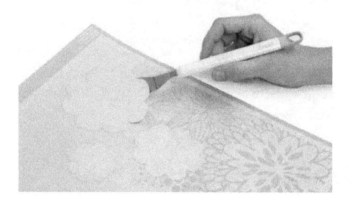

Trimmer

The Cricut 12 "portable trimmer with 15" swing arm helps you cut or mark straight lines with precision. Replacement blade storage compartments at the bottom make new blades easily accessible on the go.

Marker Pen The Cricut Marker Pen lets you use your Cricut Explore or Cricut Maker machine to mark fold lines for cards and envelopes, boxes, 3D projects, and more. The machines hold the Marking Pen and a cutting blade at the same time, so you can cut and mark in one step, without changing the mats.

Accessories

TrueControl Knife

TrueControl Knife gives you better control for beautiful results on a wide range of materials, including paper, cardstock, thin plastics, tarps, fabrics, and more. It features a blade locking system for greater control, a no-touch experience to facilitate blade changing, and premium steel blades for effortless cutting. It also has a soft handle, a protective cover and a stabilizing function.

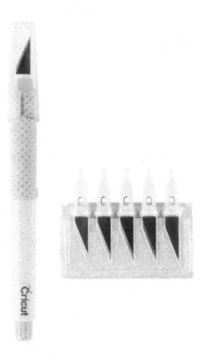

- Blade change
- Turn to unlock.
- Press the button to release the used blade into the cartridge.
- Store used blades in the cartridge.
- Align the base of the handle with a new blade.

- Press the button, then, without removing the blade from the cartridge, attach the handle to the blade. Release the button and remove the blade from the cartridge. Turn to lock.

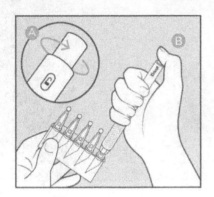

Self-healing mats

Cricut self-healing mats are double-sided and large, easy to read on a 1 "wide edge and multi-angle grids. They contain almost 2 times more self-healing material than similar competitive mats. For use with rotary cutters and blades Precision. Cricut self-healing mats come in 12 "x12", 18 "x24" and 24 "x36". They also come in three decorative patterns.

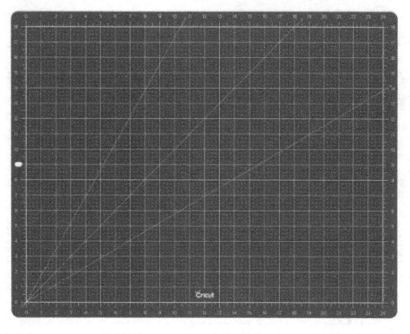

Acrylic ruler

Cricut acrylic rulers help provide complete edge-to-edge measurements for all your extra long projects.

They have a frosted finish with easy-to-read measurements on light and dark materials, with measurement marks in 1/8 "increments and lines at 30, 45 and 60 degree angles.

Cricut acrylic rulers come in 3 different sizes: 3 "x 18", 6 "x 26", and 12 "x 24".

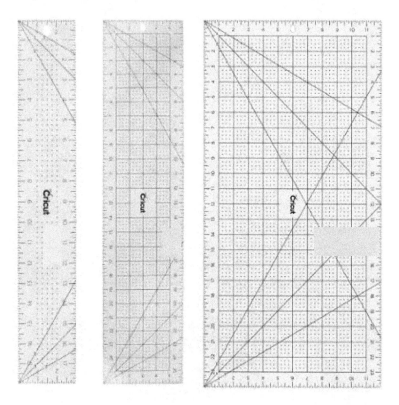

Rotary cutter

Cricut rotary cutters make it easy to cut fabric by hand. A comfortable, symmetrical grip gives you precise control whether right or left handed. It also features a quick-release blade holster for safety when not in use. Cricut rotary cutters come in 45mm and 60mm.

Cutting rule

This 18 "aluminum cutting ruler has a rigid stainless steel surface and dual directional laser engraved measurement marks. Protection guards hands from sharp cutting tools. Anti-slip textured base controls work surface to give you security and control.

Fabric Craft Set

Ideal companions for cutting fabrics with your Cricut Maker!

Fabric

Scissors Cricut 8 "fabric scissors provide clean, defined cuts on leather, denim and multiple layers of fabric. They are made of stainless steel and have a comfortable handle for left and right handed users.

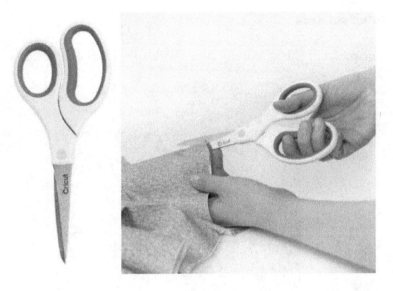

Seam ripper

Removes seams and small stitches with ease and precision.

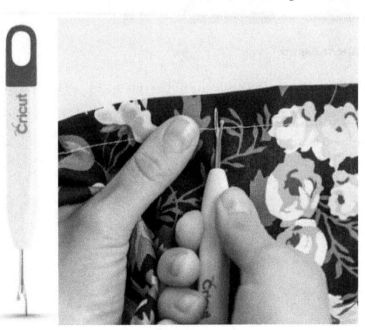

Fiber scissors

The perfect tool for cutting fibers with speed and ease

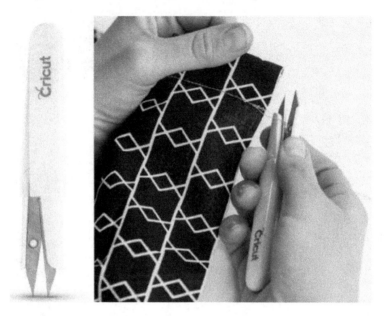

Tape measure

The Cricut tape measure measures up to 60 inches in the flexible material making it ideal for fabric and other items that have no straight lines or edges.

Pincushion and pins

Store and easily access pins for your fabric projects.

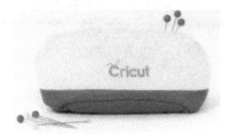

Leather

Thimble protect your fingers when sewing by hand with this leather thimble.

Wide nose pliers

A fundamental tool to remove fabric from your FabricGrip mats.

Roller

The Cricut Roller firmly adheres material to your cutting mat and is perfect for pressing fabric, vinyl or heat-adhesive vinyl, as well as inking pads for making prints.

Paper Craft Set

The tools paper crafts help make beautiful paper creations, creations including cards, scrapbooks, holidays, home decorations and much more.

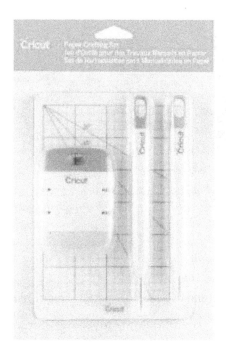

Punch

The Punch allows you precise placement of fine cuts and trims.

Filigree

Tool The filigree tool makes smooth, closed decorative spirals.

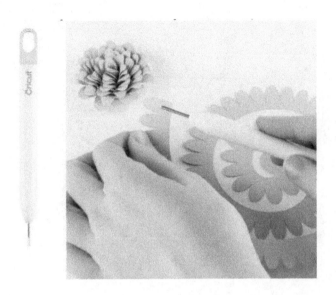

Edge Aging Edge

Aging creates the effect of textured edges on paper.

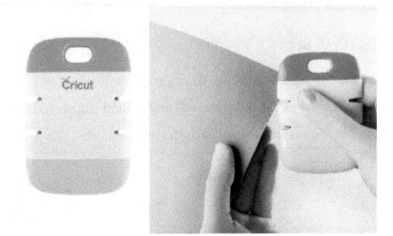

Craft

Mat The Craft Mat features multi-purpose perforations and self-healing surfaces.

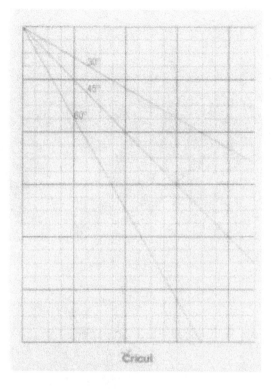

Vinyl Craft Set

Use this set of specialized weeding tools to make it easy to remove excess material from inside and around your vinyl and heat-adhesive vinyl cuts and even the toughest cuts.

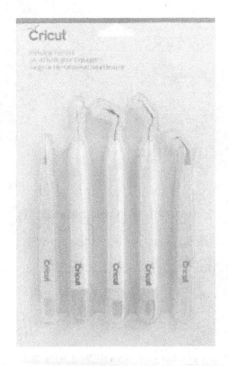

Fine nose pliers

Hook tip forceps

Escardillo

Drilling tool

Latest Tools for Cricut Maker

Cricut has just announced four new tools for Cricut Maker. As we already knew, one of the advantages of the Maker is what they called the "Adaptive Tool System" which promised to develop a lot of new tools to use with the machine. And so it is being.

The first thing to keep in mind is that the four new tools that are going to be released will be mounted on the Quick Swap Housing , or "Quick Change Bracket", which is the same bracket that scoring wheel uses. If you have the scoring wheel you will know that changing the head is as easy as changing a blade, so there are no complications. Therefore, you can use all the new tools with a single support and, if you already have the scoring wheel, you will not need to buy another one.

And having said that, we are going to see the 4 new heads.

Drilling blade

One of the advantages of the adaptive tool system is the ability to use rotary blades. Until now we had the normal rotary knife, but now two new models will arrive. First, the drill, or dotted line. What this blade does is cut broken lines and leave bonding points on the paper, the typical dotted line that is then used to break. This is very practical for making tickets, packaging that can later be opened ... Considering that Cricut Design Space did not give us the option of cutting dotted lines, this new tool is a great advance when it comes to making designs.

As a technical detail, say that they will be 2.5mm cut lines and 0.5mm uncut holes. Perfect to later throw and cut into a lot of materials: paper, cardboard, rubber, acetate.

Wave blade

Another typical model of circular blades is wave cutting. In this way we achieve a different finish on our cuts with minimal effort.

The wave knife will turn our straight lines into a subtle zigzag, and that can come in handy, for example, when creating a card edge or giving a different finish to any project.

I remind you that these two heads, although they are rotating blades, will not be mounted on the support of the rotating blade but on that of the scoring wheel.

Debossing tip

This is what we normally call "embossing tip" but it is actually called "debossing" because "embossing" is the relief up and "debossing" is down. In this case, since the tip is going to press on the paper, it will make the relief to the bottom and, therefore, it is called a debossing instead of embossing tip.

The advantage of these tips is that when using it in our cutting plotter, we can make a totally personalized design. Unlike other systems like the Big Shot, which work with folders, in this case, we will have total freedom of design. We will have to see how the finish is. Emboss always works best on soft or thick surfaces so it will be an ideal match for foil cardstock, thick papers, feather board and even balsa wood!

Engraving tip

Finally, they have taken out the metal engraving tip that we have been waiting for so long. With this tip we can engrave on metal plates. With the strength of the Maker it is likely that we can record on something more than aluminum or tin, but it will still have to be seen in operation to know it. On the other hand, it can also be used on other materials such as wood, methacrylate, plastic or leather. It is ideal for making pet tags, engraving key chains, creating commemorative plaques ... And many more things that we are sure will come up with.

Cricut Basics for Beginners

Using Quick Mode

Quick Mode is a feature of the Cricut Explore Air 2 and Cricut Maker machines that lets you cut and write up to twice as fast as previous Cricut Explore models. This feature is available with the Vinyl, Transfer and Cardstock material settings (Vinyl to Cardstock + on the Explore Smart Set dial). Look here the findings of comparative tests.

- When you are ready to write and / or cut your project, proceed to the Cut screen.
- The Quick Mode option is available if you select the applicable material.
- To activate Quick Mode, simply click / tap the switch to position it "on".

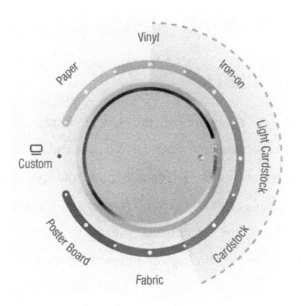

Choosing material parameters

We've tested hundreds of materials with the Cricut Explore and Cricut Maker machines to help you make the projects of your dreams come true without surprises. Choosing a material setting for your cutouts is easy!

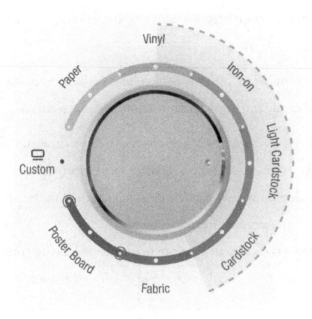

The Cricut Explore Smart Set dial is a material selection dial that offers presets for best results on paper, vinyl, transfers, cardstock, fabric, poster board, and more. The Smart Set dial eliminates the need for manual pressure, depth and speed adjustments. Just turn the dial to your material type and press the Go button!

Custom Materials

The Cricut Explore and Cricut Maker machines can cut all kinds of materials and we've added a long list of pre-programmed settings to Design Space to give you great flexibility when working with different materials for your projects. You can choose from these pre-programmed settings or even create your own!

Select a platform below for step-by-step instructions on using, creating and modifying or deleting custom material settings.

1. Log into Design Space and create / open a project.
2. Make sure your Cricut Maker or Cricut Explore machine is turned on and connected to your computer.
3. Go to the project preview screen.
4. If you have a Cricut Explore machine, make sure your Smart Set dial is set to Custom .

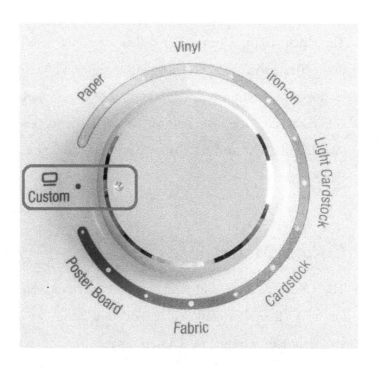

5. Select Browse All Materials .

Moving the star wheels

The little white rings on the round bar of your Cricut Maker machine are called star wheels. These wheels prevent material from moving during cutting, especially for the Print, Then Cut function. The wheels can, however, leave marks on thick materials (eg leather, felt and foam paper).

Before making a cut on these materials, and before any cut with the knife blade, bring the star wheels to the far right of the round bar. For that, proceed as following :

1. If the cart is in the middle, turn off your machine, then gently move it to either side until you have enough room to move the star wheels.

2. Take a star wheel between your thumb and forefinger and, with light pressure, gently push it towards the large rubber rollers, located to the right of the round bar. Repeat this for each wheel.

3. When cutting thinner material, replace the star wheels, spacing them evenly (approximately 5.6 cm (2.2 ")).

Note : **Firmer** pressure may be needed the first time you move the star wheels. While replacing the wheels, hold the machine with one hand to stabilize it.

Tip: When on the side, the star wheels partially cover the cutting area of your mat. It is therefore recommended that you cut the material leaving only about 2.5 cm (1 ") on the right side of the belt; this will prevent material from passing under the star wheels as the belt moves through the machine.

Replacing accessory holder

The accessory holder is pre-installed in the Accessory Holder A. However, if you need to remove and replace it, follow these steps:

Note: It is not necessary to remove the accessory holder to insert a scratching pen or stylus.

1. Open the Accessory Holder A.
2. Place your thumb under the accessory holder and exert upward pressure while pushing the holder down. The adapter will be ejected from the accessory holder.

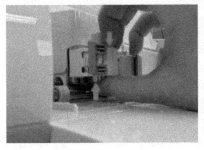 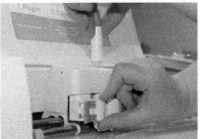

3. To reinstall the accessory holder, place a thumb under Support A to stabilize it while you insert the accessory holder as above.
4. When inserting, exert some pressure. The accessory holder snaps into the correct position when properly installed.

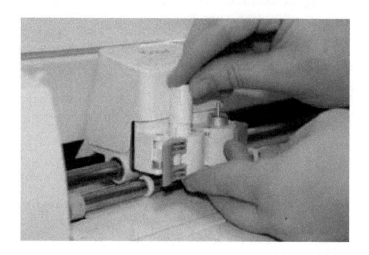

Note: The accessory holder for the Explore One machine is different from that for the Explore, Explore Air, Explore Air 2, and Cricut Maker machines. In the Explore One machine, the accessory holder switches with the blade holder when the user wishes to write or scratch. In the Explore, Explore Air, Explore Air 2 and Cricut Maker machines, the accessory holder is housed in its own holder, independent of the blade holder.

Using Mobile Device Charging Part

The Cricut Maker has a standard 5 Volt charge port at the bottom of the machine on the right side. You can use this port to charge your mobile device while cutting!

Important: The device may not charge if you are using the Cricut Explore power cable. It is therefore recommended to use the power cable supplied with your Cricut Maker machine.

Note: This port is only for charging mobile devices. It is not configured for data transfer.

Installing Bluetooth adapter

Note: Cricut Maker, Explore Air, and Explore Air 2 machines have a built-in Bluetooth connection. They therefore do not need an adapter.

1. Power on the Cricut Explore or Explore One machine.
2. Remove the cap from the Bluetooth adapter.
3. Insert the adapter into the Explore machine (Cricut text face up).

About two-thirds of the adapter fits into the machine.

When the end of the adapter lights up blue, it cannot be pushed any further. The adapter is installed correctly.

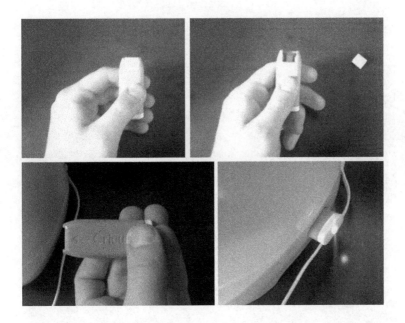

Important: Be sure to remove the Bluetooth adapter before placing the Cricut Explore machine in the tote or its carry bag. The adapter protrudes from the machine and could break or sink into the machine, possibly damaging the adapter itself and / or the machine's Bluetooth port.

Machine Serial Number Location

The serial number of your Cricut machine is shown on the label affixed to the bottom of the machine. In the case of old machines, it is directly indicated under the barcode.

The serial number is a 12-character alphanumeric code.

The serial number begins with the following letter:

o Explore - E

o Explore Air - A

o Explore One - I

o Explore Air 2 - S

o Maker – Q

Cricut Design Space Options

- In **Templates** you can choose between several elements, arranged in categories, prepared for you to use as a reference base to place your designs at the correct size. They will not be saved in your project.

- **Projects:** you can find in addition to your projects that are saved in the cloud, complete works ready to cut or sketch, you have some free for you to try.

- **Images:** You have hundreds of resources ready to cut or print and cut. Many are free.

- **Text: you** just have to write what you want and select the font and size.

- **Shapes:** you can choose some basic to use in your projects.

Cricut Design Space.

Load images

1. In the upload section, you can import images or fillings into your project. Images must be **jpg, gif, png, bmp, svg or dxf** files.

2. Press upload image, select it in the folder and press open. Now you must select the complexity of the image to trace it, in our case it is a simple image with a single color and transparent background. Press continue.

3. Now you can see a preview where you can edit the previous result reducing colors or tolerance or deleting parts directly with the magic wand.

4. Press continue and you will reach the last screen where you must choose if you want to print and cut the image or if you are only going to cut it as in our case. You can

write some tags to easily find the images later. Press save.

5. Now we can see it in the uploaded images, click on it and click on "insert image" and it will appear on our canvas.

6. On the right the layers appear, you can select them and choose what you want the maker to do with them: draw, mark, record, cut ... You can also hide or delete them.

7. Now resize the design to your liking and hit the top right on **Do it** .

8. On this screen you can select the size of the material and in our case as we are going to cut textile vinyl we will use the mirror mode. Click continue.

9. In this step you must select the material, select from the multiple predefined ones. You can also create custom materials.

10. Once the material is selected, it will appear which blade you should choose.

11. Place the blade holder on the carriage by pulling the gray tab, put the blade down completely and close the tab again.

12. Place the material on the mat. We have chosen the blue light grip.

13. Load the mat by pressing the advance key and press the Cricut key to start **cutting**.

Cricut Projects for Beginners

Wedding Table Plan

Completion time: more than 2 hours.

Difficulty: 1/3

To make your plant wedding table plan, you will need:

- Cricut Machine

- 1 box of 25 Pollen sheets 210x297 mm 210g - Ivory

- Extra strong double-sided adhesive tape - 6mm x 10m -

- High temperature glue gun -

- White metal ring 25 cm -

- Straight scissors 17 cm -

- 1 natural kraft string -

Discover all the steps below:

STEP 1/13 Using the cricut, cut multiple sheets using the different shades of green card stock.

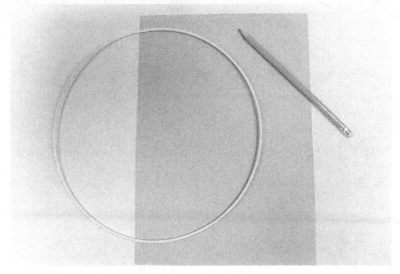

STEP 2/13 Trace the inner and outer outline of the half of the ring on green card stock with a pencil, and cut out the half moon, leaving enough room on both sides to be able to fold it around the ring.

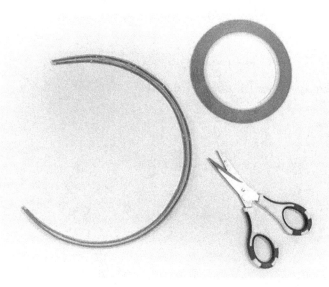

STEP 3/13 Stick the double-sided adhesive tape on the half-moon.

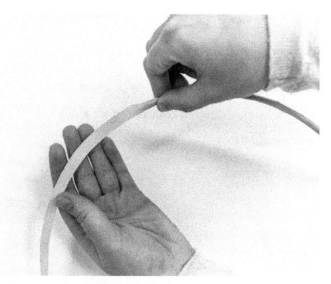

STEP 4/13 Fold it around half of the hoop, pinching the edges so that they are secure. This edge will serve as a base for easily gluing your paper sheets.

STEP 5/13 Arrange the different cut sheets on the part of the ring covered with paper and glue the elements with a glue gun.

STEP 6/13 Using the cricut and the Natural Leaves die, cut the berries out of the cream card stock.

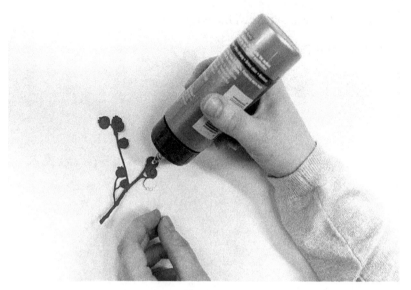

STEP 7/13 Glue the berries on the corresponding branches of the set to bring out the berries.

STEP 8/13 Insert and glue the berry branches among the other leaves where you want to add shades of color.

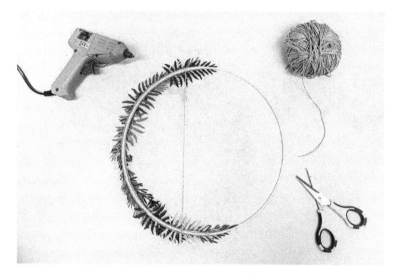

STEP 9/13 Tie the string to the back of the metal ring with the glue gun, cut off the excess if necessary

STEP 10/13 Print the table numbers on the cream card stock, cut out in a circle and glue it on the string, towards the center of the ring.

STEP 11/13 Print the names of the guests on the cream paper and cut them out with scissors, forming banners.

STEP 12/13 Create your seating plan and paste the guest names wherever you want!

STEP 13/13 Create as many rings as there are guest tables for your wedding and arrange them on a recovered wooden pallet.

Paper Decoration

To make this tropical decoration, you will need:

- Cricut

- Set of 6 Scrapbooking paper sheets -

- Leaf - 30.5x30.5cm - petrol blue .

- Leaf - 30.5x30.5cm - menthol green

- Leaf - 30.5x30.5cm - lime green

- Leaf - 30.5x30.5cm - spring green

- Slate scrapbooking sheet - 30x30cm

- Sheet of 34 epoxy stickers -

- 8 card stock polaroid frames -

- Assortment of 40 die-cuts -

- 100m two-tone spool - Sky blue

- 16 mini clothespins 35 mm

- Vivaldi smooth sheet A4 240g - Canson - white n ° 1

- Precision cutter and 3 blades

- Blue cutting mat - 2mm - A3

- Acrylic and aluminum ruler 30cm black

- Precision scissors 13.5cm blue bi-material rings

- 3D adhesive squares

- Mahé Tools - - scrapbooking

- Pack of 6 HB graphite pencils

Preparation time: 2h

Techniques: Stencil, Collage, Origami - Folding, Tropical

Discover below all the steps to realize your summer decoration "Tropical Paradise":

1. Gather the materials.

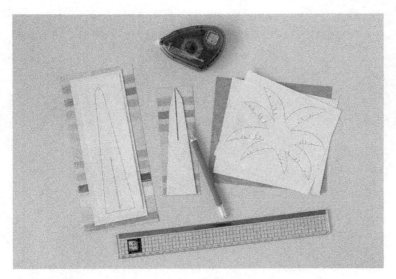

2. Using the template and a pencil, reproduce the palm tree on the papers in the collection.

3. Cut out using cricut.

4. Assemble the trunk of the palm tree. Glue the foliage. Using the template, reproduce the traces of the cocktail support on thin cardboard, following the dimensions indicated. Cover it with the collection paper.

5. After having cut in the slate sheet: 1 x (8.5 x 8.5 cm). Choose a Polaroid. Glue the slate sheet to the back of the Polaroid. Using a chalk pen, write "Cocktail of the day". Decorate with the stickers. Fold the support at the dotted lines.

6.

Using the templates and a pencil, draw the leaves and flowers on the paper and on the collection paper. Draw.

7. Choose photos. Cut them to size: 8.5 x 8.5 cm. Stick to the back of the Polaroids.

8. Glue the leaves and flowers together. Cut the string to the desired dimensions and glue it to the back of the flowers. Glue the birds on the string and hang the photos using mini clips.

And here is a pretty summer and tropical decoration! Beautiful evenings in perspective!

Crepe Paper Flowers

Completion time: more than 2 hours

Difficulty: 1/3

To make this bouquet of crepe paper flowers, you will need:

- Assortment of 10 rolls of crepe paper

Or discover our range of crepe papers

- 20 thread stems with flower 1mm x 50 cm

- Vvinyl glue

- 4 pairs of multi-use scissors

- Cutout template to download, print and cut.

Find all the detailed steps below:

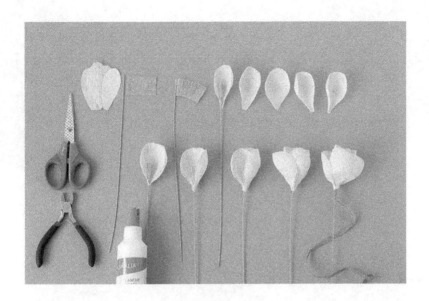

1. Creation of yellow flowers:

Print the template and cut it out on Cricut. Cut 5 petals out of yellow florist crepe paper. Be sure to place the vertical template in the direction of the grooves of the crepe paper. Cut a 2.5 x 5 cm strip of orange florist crepe paper. Bisect a binding wire with a clamp cutting.

Stretch each petal by placing your thumbs in the middle of the petals. Dig with your thumbs apart. The petals become very rounded. Finely notch the orange strip. Paste up the binding wire and winding the paper to form the pistils.

Stick the pistils in the hollow of a first petal. Glue the second petal slightly offset by about 3mm. Glue all the petals until they half cover the first petal. Pinch the basis for refining.

Cut a strip of green crepe paper about 0.5 x 15 cm long. Shoot it. Glue one end to the base of the petals. Apply glue and wrap it tightly around the rod. Leave to dry. Prepare 10 yellow flowers like this.

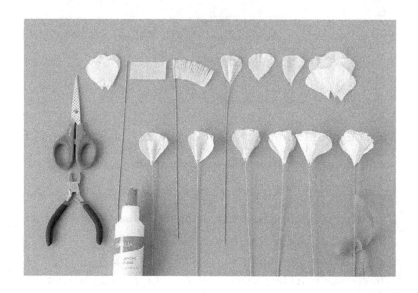

2. Creation of white:

Cut 10 petals out of white florist crepe paper . Be sure to place the vertical template in the direction of the grooves of the crepe paper. Cut a 2.5 x 5 cm strip of yellow florist crepe paper. Cut a wire to be tied in half using wire cutters.

Pinch the top edge of a petal starting from the left and spacing the inches 2 millimeters apart. Stretch the paper. Move your thumbs and repeat the operation every 5 millimeters, to form little ruffles. Do the same for each petal. Place thumbs in the middle of the petals. Dig lightly with your thumbs apart without completely stretching the paper. Finely notch the yellow strip. Stick the top of the binding wire and winding the paper to form the pistils.

Stick the pistils in the hollow of a first petal. Glue the second petal offset by about 5 millimeters. Glue all the petals by rolling the petals to surround the flower several times. Pinch the base to refine it.

Cut a strip of green crepe paper about 0.5 x 15 cm long. Shoot it. Glue one end to the base of the petals. Apply glue and wrap it tightly around the rod. Let dry. Prepare and 10 white flowers.

3. Creating peony flowers:

Cut 7 petals of the first template out of bright pink florist crepe paper. Prepare 7 heart-shaped petals and 6 large petals and 5 sepals in green crepe paper . Sure to place the template vertical in the direction of paper grooves crepe.

Cut a 3.5 x 11 cm strip of orange florist crepe paper . Cut into both a binding wire with a clamp cutting.

Stretch the orange strip. Fold it in 3 and cut. Finely notch each orange strip . Glue the first strip to the top of the wire to be bound and roll up the paper to form the pistils. Add the second, then the third strip. Spread the pistils to give them volume. Pinch the base to refine it.

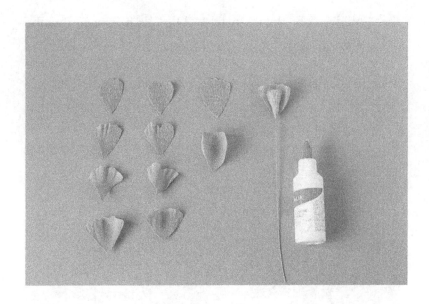

4. Give the form to the petals:

Take the first set of petals. Pinch the top edge of a petal starting from the left and spacing the inches 2 millimeters apart. Stretch the paper. Move your thumbs and repeat the operation every 5 millimeters, to form little ruffles. Do the same for each petal. Place thumbs in the middle of the petals. Widen slightly, keeping inch without fully extend the paper.

Prepare the same way the petals in a heart shape.

For larger petals, stretch them one by one. Place thumbs in the middle of the petals. Dig with your thumbs apart. The petals become very rounded.

Stick the pistils in the hollow of a first petal.

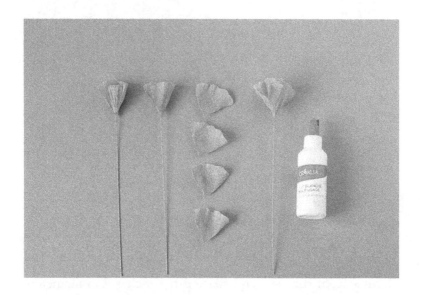

Step 5.

Glue the second petal offset by about 5 millimeters. Glue by wrapping the first 7 petals to surround the flower several times. Pinch the base to refine it.

Step 6:

Glue the second set of heart- shaped petals onto the flower. Glue each petal a little higher than the base, on the first petals to create a more garnished effect . Paste wrapping around the petals of the flower.

Finish by gluing the last set of 6 rounded petals, arranging to surround the flower only once.

Step 7.

Turn the flower over and glue the sepals starting from the stem to cover the base of the flower. Cut a strip of green crepe paper about 0.4 x 15 cm long . Shoot it. Glue it to the base of the sepals. Apply glue and wrap it tightly around the rod. Let dry. Prepare 5 hot pink peonies and 4 soft pink peonies in this way .

Step 8. The foliage.

Print the template and cut it out using cricut. Cut 10 leaves from green florist crepe paper . Be sure to place the vertical template in the direction of the grooves of the crepe paper. Cut a wire to be tied in half using wire cutters. Paste the wire bonding at the center of the foliage.

Cut a strip of green crepe paper about 0.4 x 15 cm long. Shoot it. The paste to the base of the foliage. Apply glue and wrap it tightly around the rod . Let dry. Prepare 10 green leaves in this way.

Floral Letter In Watercolor

Time: 60 minutes.

To make your floral letter in watercolor, you will need:

-Cricut Maker

- Box of 12 Aqua pencils

- 3 watercolor brushes

- Watercolor pad 25 x 25 cm

- 200 Double-sided adhesive foam squares - Créalia

- Extra strong double-sided adhesive tape - 6mm x 10m - Créalia

- Template to download and print.

Find all the steps:

STEP 1/9 Print the templates and using the tracing paper, reproduce the letter chosen on the watercolor paper as well as the flowers.

STEP 2/9 Color the letter with watercolor pencils. Make areas darker to create contrast

STEP 3/9 Apply water to the entire letter with a watercolor brush

STEP 4/9 Color the plants. For flowers, put different colors on the petals

STEP 5/9 With the watercolor brush, apply water and blend the colors together

STEP 6/9 For the foliage, apply a first color and add lines of different colors to create nuances

STEP 7/9 Cut out the patterns using Cricut maker.

STEP 8/9 Glue the patterns on the letter using the foam squares. Then glue everything on the canvas with double-sided tape.

STEP 9/9 Your floral monogram is ready.

Paper Fans

The necessary equipment :

- Circuit Maker

- A4 papers

- Round scalloped perforator 7.5 cm

- Punch Round 3.8cm

- Double-sided

- Mini high temperature glue gun

The stages of the realization:

1. Fold a sheet of A4 paper accordion lengthwise in Cricut maker. Repeat for 2 more sheets of paper.

2. Fold the accordions in half in the middle.

3. Add double-sided tape to the ends

4. Secure the parts together. You must have 3 identical parts.

5. Glue the 3 parts together with double-sided tape to form the pennant.

6. Cut circles using circuit from colored or patterned paper using a scalloped circle hole punch.

7. Glue the circles in the center of each pennant using the glue gun.

8. Repeat the operation with a smaller round hole punch. You can create larger diameter flags by gluing 2 A4 sheets together in the longest part of the paper beforehand to form A3 paper.

9. Create several fans by varying sizes to decorate your party atmosphere.

Thankyou Box

- The Cricut Machine

- Color papers

- Glue

- Removable golden vinyl

- Gold Marker

- The template

- The typos used are Courrier new and Adalaide (the latter is from Cricut)

- For those who can log into Cricut, here is the Design Space project link .

Discover all the steps below:

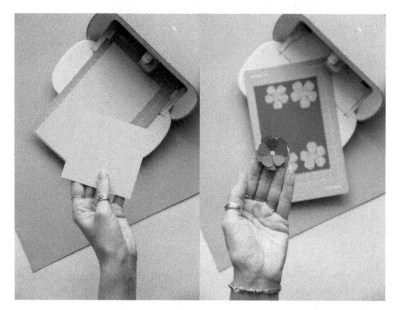

Step 1 / Using your application prepare the cutting of your paper templates for your box, as well as the paper decorations (ex: foliage / flowers / hearts).

Step 1 BIS / Using your application prepare the cutting of your paper templates for your box, as well as the paper decorations (ex: leaves / flowers / hearts).

Step 2 / Prepare the cutting of your heart stickers with your SMART VINYL REMOVABLE Gold paper which you will use to close your box.

Step 3 / Now that the paper templates are cut out, use your GOLD marker to create and draw your texts. You can choose to write whatever you want.

Step 4 / It's time to stick your papers on your cardboard box. The "Thank you" paper is to be placed inside the box on the upper part. Also place your plain pink paper template at the bottom of your box.

Step 4 bis / Now stick your paper with your text "Just for you" on the outside of the box.

Step 5 / Come and create your floral arrangement inside your box using strong glue, I decided to add a real craspedia to it so that I don't just have paper. If not, you can add a branch of eucalyptus, or olive tree.

Step 6 / Once your interior decoration is finished, you can now close your box and seal it with your golden heart stickers. All you have to do is offer them.

Tips of Making Money Using Cricut

Before you start trying to make money from your Cricut, take some time to think about whether or not it really is what you want to do. When I bought Cricut, I thought about starting a personalization and stationery business, but everything in life is trial and error, I am still in the testing phase.

Here are some things to think about before "launching":

- Are you doing it just because your friends say your creations are amazing?

- Do you want to support your family financially?

- Are you doing it for some extra money?

- Are you willing to deal with HARD customers? (there are always difficult clients)

- Do you want to turn your hobby into a job?

- Can you learn more about marketing on and off the network?

- Do you have enough time and space to start a small business?

- Do you like to make crafts with your Cricut? So much to do over and over again?

I definitely don't want to discourage you from starting to make money from your Cricut, but you have to put your feet on the ground and I also want you to **be smart about it** . Your answers to these questions do not necessarily determine your decision whether to launch or not, BUT they will help you realize what it will be like for you to start a small business with your Cricut.

All about copyright

Since you decided to get into this business, we should talk about licenses and copyrights, as this is the area where you can get into trouble the fastest. And the question why ?, because all the images, cut files that you download or even copies from the Internet were created by someone, and the simple fact of finding them on

Google does not give you the right to reproduce it or worse, sell it on the Internet.

There are different policies that protect images, below I describe the most common.

Cricut angel policy

Within the same Cricut Design Space system there is a library of Cricut images to create with the machine. You can create and sell with such designs but under the "Cricut Angel" Policy . Please read this policy carefully , you will find many things there, Some things it mentions:

- Most Cricut Access images are included in this policy.

- Create up to 10,000 items to sell using Cricut images.

- Don't just sell individual images.

- You must include a copyright notice with your projects.

- Do not include licensed content, such as images from Disney or Marvel.

PERSONAL USE VS. COMMERCIAL USE

If you prefer to use very specific images, you can buy them in online stores. Don't just download them from Google images and put them in your projects... It is very likely that if you do, you are violating copyrights.

When purchasing images online, be sure to read the file's terms of use. Most of these images only include a personal use license, that is, you cannot create products to sell with these types of files. There may also be the option to buy the same image but with a commercial license, just remember to read the terms.

There are images of licensed characters that normally belong to Disney and / or Marvel, such as (and this will surprise you as much as I do): Elsa from Frozen or Iron Man from Marvel. Using these images is breaking copyright and you may have trouble using it as a way to make money. My advice would be to stay away from using these images, it can bring you an ugly problem and even a lawsuit or fine.

Starting a Cricut craft business

Now that we are clear on the Legal topic, let's talk about how to earn money and get the best out of your Cricut.

DEFINE YOUR NICHE

One of the worst things you can do is do whatever people ask you to do. A glass here, a personalization over there, a cake topper from today to tomorrow. You'll end up with lower margins than the market, perhaps wasted product and a confused audience.

I recommend defining your niche and type of product to one or very few elements and / or themes so that you can have a strong and your audience can remember you faster. When deciding what type of products to sell, consider "added value." This can be additional things to your product or just perfect it. In this way you could charge a "premium" price.

BUY MATERIALS IN LARGE QUANTITIES

Having decided on your niche, you can buy your supplies and materials, what I call "wholesale". This is nothing more than buying large quantities, say 10 foot vinyl rolls, boxes of 10 glasses or cups at cheaper prices than if you buy them per unit. Cricut also sells wholesale materials.

QUALITY REALLY MATTERS

One of the fastest ways to destroy your business is to produce a low-quality product. Word of mouth travels faster than we think, and the worst part is that you can't change the ratings you get if you're selling your product in an online store.

Therefore, when you are creating your business, make sure you can consistently produce quality products. If you understand that your quality is falling because you are not in control because you receive many requests, consider seeking help or stopping your orders for a short time.

Whatever you do, do it well.

How to set the price

It bothers me to see people selling their beautiful super elaborate creations at SO cheap prices. Those people are not even valuing their own time. They are not taking into account your talent, materials or many other things that are important when setting prices.

Monetizing your art

You have practiced, perfected and established a style of that art that you like to do so much. You have decorated cards, personalized objects, created pictures with motivational phrases; and with pride you have shared your work on social networks.

Now comes the question that scares you so much. "What would you charge to do THIS?" It is super exciting and flattering to know that there are people who ask you to do what you love to earn money.

However, as exciting as it is, it scares us, and a LOT. To be honest I still feel nervous when sending a quote to my clients. We have all been there on several occasions, and I know it is difficult at first, but the most important thing is to have everything in order.

Before you start thinking about monetizing your art, you should realize all the factors that you may not have considered when valuing your work. Believe it or not, there are many more reasons behind the prices, apart from "because that is what so-and-so charges." Alright then let's get started.

SOMEONE WANTS TO HIRE ME .. WHAT DO I DO NOW?

Congratulations! You must be super excited, but before responding with a price, or worse, offering to do it for free , there is a lot to consider when evaluating your work, and I hope I'm covering a large part here.

Why is pricing so important? Shouldn't I feel good just by putting the price that I understand "correct"? Well, it is not wrong to ask yourself this question, however you must be sure that you are not bothering yourself, the client and other artists in the business.

When you are self-employed, you are in charge of the money you earn, so you want to do it right. It is important that you ask yourself these questions before setting a price.

How much is your time and energy worth to you?
How does your experience compare to others in the

business?

What are your material costs?

What is the size of the project?

What is the project deadline?

Are you going to include shipping, or charge extra?

Is this piece going to be original, or is the customer making and selling multiple copies?

Does the client want you to convert the artwork into a digital format?

Will you be creating the artwork in your own studio or on-site?

What will be your minimum charge for small jobs?

YOUR TIME + ENERGY

This is where the wellness factor comes in, where you need to think about how much your time is worth to you. It's worth a lot more than buying the cheapest combo at McDonald's, but there the questions come... Karissa, how much exactly? How do i find out It is difficult to answer the frank but there are certain guidelines that I can tell you that can help you.

The typical answer is that you put yourself a monthly salary with which you feel comfortable, I will speak in an imaginary way based on some local statistics of the Dominican Republic to speak with numbers and you can understand. Let's say (I made it up) that on average a monthly salary in my country is $ 15,000 Dominican pesos and this is the number with which you value your time and energy.

This number will be divided by 4.3, this number is established as the average of weeks in the year since there are months that have 30 days, another 31 and February with 28. Already starting to see the difference? Now try to use that math to calculate your own hourly rate.

Start with the monthly salary you feel comfortable with:

_____

Divide that number by 4.3 and put it here: _____

Now divide this other number by 44 (remember that this number may vary). So this result is your hourly rate that you will put here: _____

YOUR LEVEL OF EXPERIENCE

You may have been practicing or creating for a week or a year before being asked about working for money. This is more about the quality of your work, rather than how long you've been at it. BUT EYE: It is not that you are going to compare with artists who have a level of professionalism for a long time, it is a matter of an objective perspective.

Is it clean? Is consistent? Do you have your own style? Do you feel confident in your work? Have you taken workshops or courses to ensure your techniques are correct?

COST OF MATERIALS

Are you using cheap store markers or artist quality paints? Do you use expensive papers and prepared inks? Are they special items you need? Do you have to order online that are specific to some part of the world or available near you?

The value increases with the quality of your tools and materials, as well as your knowledge of them. If you answer "What kind of paint do you have / do you use?" With a "I don't know ... I've had it for a long time and the label it has is no longer visible" or "a friend gave it to me and I don't know where it got it "Your work will not be as valuable as that of someone whose answer is" I use Winsor and Newton's lightweight, water-resistant watercolors. "

Artist-quality materials cost more, so it's important that you know the cost of your materials in case they run out.

Also, for a big job, you may have to burn seven special markers. That is a part of the cost that you do not want out of your time or pocket, but is an expense that must be included in your estimate.

Of course, if in a job you used only part of the material, obviously you are not going to charge the full cost of that material, there you must use mathematics, knowing in advance how much of the material you used and obtaining a percentage.

PROJECT SIZE

This is probably one of the first factors to value your project. How big is it? Creating something, for example a lettering composition is an 8 ½ x 11 inch sheet with ten words will take much less time and less materials than those same ten words on an 8x10 foot board. You can have a price for measurements, let's say square inches or better use your hourly rate that we work above.

DELIVERY / SHIPPING

You must indicate in your budget if the delivery is included or is an extraordinary payment. That means you need to know where the piece is going. You may have to purchase parcel shipping quotes outside of your city based on the weight size and service you really need. I recommend that you investigate the rates of the shipping companies and thus have a standard shipping cost.

ORIGINAL OR CONTINUOUS USE?

Will your client use your art once (like a wedding card), continuously (like a business card or blog), or multiple times (like a T-shirt to resell)? It is always a good idea to ask this question in advance. The answer will help you determine how valuable your artwork is to the customer. If it will be used continuously to promote or generate direct income for your client, the value increases.

DELIVERABLES

What should you deliver to your customer as a finished product? An original art? Or is it digital? Both of them? What file formats? JPG, PNG, TIF, EPS, AI? Do you have experience digitizing, and do you have the best tools to do it?

Spending time digitizing and preparing multiple files takes time and experience, and therefore should be priced accordingly. There are also those printed from digital art. Will you mail the file? In a memory? Digital start and then you delivered it printed? All this must be taken into account considering the time and effort it took to do it. NOTE: a digital job is even more expensive since it can be reproduced and using specialized programs requires previous experience and learning, which I suppose also cost you to acquire it.

LOCATION (IN OR OUT OF YOUR STUDIO)

Your hourly rate will also largely depend on where you will be doing the work.

When you have the luxury of your own space you can perform several tasks at the same time, that is, you can be working on two projects at the same time. This makes it easy to access all of your supplies and materials. The most convenient way for you to work in your own place, at your own pace with everything you need at hand, you should not worry about traffic.

If the job requires you to be somewhere outside your study (let's say a restaurant for example), the value of your time will increase significantly. You will have to travel to and from the place (which needs to be included in your work time), carry all your materials with you and only commit to that work during the assigned hours. That also means that you will be in an uncontrolled environment, this includes distractions, noise and curious people. It can be a lot of fun working on site, and it can be a real headache.

Sometimes a combination of time in your studio and on-site works best. You can carry out all the designs and preparatory work in the studio, so that you are ready to carry out your duties once you arrive on site. This would be shown as two separate hourly rates in the quote, breaking down your activities, so your client knows how they are investing their money in you.

PROJECT TERM

Only you know what time is most comfortable for you to work. If not, I recommend measuring the time you take doing your work to have an estimate and also a space in case something unforeseen occurs. If a client comes out of nowhere with a crazy panic because they are the most important in the world, ALWAYS add a fee for speed, clarifying the time it takes you in normal time for similar works, and that you will make an exception for him / her. Normally these prices vary between 50% or 100% of the labor price.

It is best to avoid these types of jobs because you start to get used to the client, only accept these cases if it is strictly necessary.

YOUR MINIMUM PRICE

You have heard the expression "I am not going to get out of bed for less than 1,000 pesos per hour." That is what we have to calculate. What hourly rate makes the project worth your time, energy and experience, in addition to cover any expenses or wear and tear on your supplies?

If someone asks you to do a tiny job, like "write my name", you need to be prepared with your minimum load. Sure, you will not charge her a price per name on invitation (say $ 50) and she would leave it like that.

Taking into account the time it will take to contact so-and-so for details (style, color, size, delivery, etc.), the time required to assemble your materials and to prepare your work space (remove the dishes from the dining room table by example , and send or deliver the final piece, $ 50 is not close to cover your time, energy and materials.